SOUL DROPS

*Poetry
and
Prose*

*by
Katherine Woodward*

Published in the United States
ISBN 978-0-9864364-2-0

About the author

1981 Katherine Woodward immigrated to the USA from the former Soviet Union where she was practicing law for a few years.

Living in NYC she was able to follow her true passion and keep up with her studies, acquiring invaluable knowledge in physiology, anatomy and the human psyche, while working in the field of medical diagnostics. In 1996 she became a certified consulting hypnotherapist. Another dream of hers came true!

In 1999 Katherine moved to the beautiful city of Sarasota. Here she continued and pursued another passion of hers: dancing and fitness.

Now, as an author, dancer and Yoga/Pilates/Dance instructor, Katherine strives to be a dedicated servant to her readers, students and clients, and to the principles of excellence in her life and career.

Preface

You honor me by reading this.
The book is tiny but its scope is at least four decades of my life. As many other people change, I also changed a lot during this time…
My *Soul Drops* reflects this change. Some of the drops are written in a different country and in a different language since I did not know English back then.
Recently I decided to put all the pieces together. I translated those that were written in Russian and placed them in the book on the page to the right of each original. They do not rhyme, but I did my best to preserve the meaning and the emotional matrix of each drop. They all are very dear to me, and maybe you will find a reflection of your own soul drops in mine...

Dedication

To the brilliant mind and stunning beauty of my parents, who set up the highest bar for me.
And to those kind souls who appeared on my way from time to time stretching their hand of help to me.

Шали

Мы как будто бы просто знакомы,
Нет уже ни любви ни огня.
Лишь незримые шали былого
Обвивают тебя и меня.
Эти шали навязчего колют,
Заставляя всмотреться туда,
Где в прощаньи с улыбкой и болью
Загорелась разлуки звезда.
Это было прощание с тобою,
С целым миром, когда то родным.
От которого в горестном море
Расстилается розовый дым...

Shawls

We are just strangers…
No more passion, no more fire…
Only the invisible shawls of the past
Are still wrapping around you and
me.
Those shawls are persistently
scratching
Pushing to look hard back in time,
Where in farewell with smile and
pain
Was shining the star of separation.
It was the farewell with you,
With the whole world, so dear once!
…And now, what is left is
 The pink smoke in the sea of sorrow.

1979

Уходя...

Уходя не хочу одного лишь,
Не оставить следа за собой,
Равнодушием душу заполнить,
Обозначиться "никакой".
Пусть ты лучше меня ненавидишь,
Пусть... что хочешь, но только след.
След глубокий и больный, словно
Слепок прожитых вместе лет...

...As I go away

As I go away, there is one thing I do not
wish;
Leave no trace behind me,
Fill your soul with indifference,
Be marked as "vestigial".
Rather anything else,
Rather just hate me,
But will there be a trace!
A trace deep and painful
Like a footprint of our years together...

1979

На берегу

Прозрачное небо повисло над морем
Подслушать его разговор.
То тучами хмурилось внемля раздорам
Сквозь волн громыхающих хор,
То солнцем блистало, смеясь врассыпную
Лучами по нежной воде.
И вновь повисало, бессменно тоскуя
По вестям в земной суете.

At the shore

Transparent sky was hovering
over the sea
Eavesdropping on his conversation.
It was frowning with dark clouds
Heeding the discords
Through the chorus of rumbling waves.
…Or It was shining with the sun,
And laughing, and scattering in bulk
Shooting it's rays into the tender water.
…And then again was hovering
over the sea,
Longing forever for more news
Of the world's vanity.

1979

Я тебя ещё не знала

Природа словно отдыхала,
Роняя в воздух тишину.
В мерцанье желтом море спало,
Скрыв задремавшую волну.
То был закат настолько нежный,
Лучами тёплыми даря...
И только жаль опять, как прежде
Со мною не было тебя...

I did not know you then

It looked like nature was resting,
Dropping quietness into the air.
In yellow glitter sea was sleeping
Hiding a dreaming wave.
That was the dusk, so tender,
Gifting with it's warm rays.
...And too bad, that again like before
 You were not with me...

1980

Я пошла с тобой

Я как тень твоей прошлой подруги
Что сейчас от тебя далеко,
Только в страшном холодном недуге
Вспоминаешь ты облик её.
…А меня полюбил ты за то лишь,
Что я очень похожа на ту.
Ну так чтож, буду рада я тоже
Если вспомнишь меня хоть в бреду…

I went with you

I am like a shadow of your ex-girlfriend
Who is far away now.
Only in a horrifying, cold sickness
Will you recall her image.
…And for me you fell only because
I remind you of her.
…So what, I will be happy
If you remember me at least
In your delirium…

1981

Лучше выпей...

От чего ты так грустно смотришь?
Сам не знаешь, как раненный пёс.
Словно боль заглушить не хочешь
От стучащих в дали колёс.
Ты припал ко времени ухом,
Ещё слышишь чего уже нет,
Ещё видишь знакомый запах,
Ещё чывствуеш кожи цвет.
И зачем в тот дождливый вечер
Нас с тобою заметил Бог?
Мягкий шепот, и руки, и плечи...
Он наверно считал что помог.
Так чего ж ты так грустно смотришь?
Не буди запорошенных дней.
Лучше выпей ещё если хочешь.
Затумань свою память о ней.

Rather have a drink...

Why the look in your eyes is so sad?
You don't even know... like a wounded
dog.
Like you don't want to dull the pain
From the sound of the wheels from
afar...
Your ear is glued to the past,
Still hear what is not there anymore...
Still see familiar smell...
Still feel the color of the skin...
...And why in that rainy evening
God was remembering us?
...Soft whisper, and hands, and
shoulders...
He probably thought he was helping...
So, why are you looking so sad?
Do not awaken those faded days.
Rather have a drink...
Blur your memory of her.

1981

Мне книжку подарил поэт

Мне книжку подарил поэт
В неё стихи свои вложил он,
И жизнь свою за много лет,
и кровь, текущую по жилам.
Кусочек сердца в ней лежит,
Душа ребёнка, мысли старца.
В ней ветер свежий шелестит
Страницами земного танца.
...А на обложке написал
Рукой своею, так, два слова.
Мне счастья в жизни пожелал
И пожелал пути большего!

The poet gifted me his book

The poet gifted me his book.
He put his rhymes in it,
His life for many years,
His blood flowing through his veins.
A piece of his heart is in it,
The soul of a child, the thoughts of a
wizard.
Fresh breeze in it rustles with the pages
of the world's dance.
…And on the cover he wrote
With his own hand, just a few words…
He wished me happiness
And he wished me a big road!

1983

Признание

Я вернусь на закате опять.
Не могу удержать свою тягу
Это томное небо понять
С облаками, несущими влагу.
С облаками что с лучшей картины сошли
И повисли в спокойствии мирном...
Я приду на закате
Объясняться в любви
Этим сгусткам дождя,
Облакам этим дивным!

Confession

I will be back at sunset again.
Can not tame my call
To understand this languid sky
With the clouds that carry moisture,
The clouds that stepped out of the best
drawing
And moving gracefully in peaceful
calmness...
...I will be back at sunset again
To confess my love
To these clusters of rain,
To these magnificent clouds!

2001

Художнику

Пределов красоты не существует,
Её многообразия не счесть.
Пусть в красках жизни ваша кисть
ликует,
В души оттенках - разум пишет свою
песнь!

To the artist

There are no limits to beauty,
Its diversity is uncountable.
Let your brush exult in the colors of life,
In the shades of the soul
let your mind write its song!

2005

Юле

В Июне солнце светит ярче,
И день приятней и теплей.
Ты рождена как луч удачи
В миру ошибок и теней.
Как "прооф" любви, которой нету
Сильнее в мире ничего,
Как стебелёк прорвавшись к свету
Сквозь глыбу камня самого.
…Твой свет теперь сильней сияет.
Ты освещаешь путь себе,
И навсегда с тобою в паре
Факел любви моей к тебе!

To Julie

In June the sun is shining brighter,
And day is warmer and more pleasant.
You were born like a ray of luck
In the world of shadows and mistakes.
Like a proof of Love
That there is nothing stronger in the
world.
Like a small stalk that broke through into
the light
Through a massive slab of stone…
…Your light is shining bolder now,
You are illuminating your own path,
And forever paired with you
The torch of my love for you.

2001

День Багодарения

Благодарю тебя за всё
За шум ручья,
За гром небесный,
За шелест листьев на ветру,
За дом родной,
За день чудестный.
За тех друзей
Что из толпы
Сумели выдти без опаски,
За голос правды
Что всегда хранит меня
С тобою в связке.
За Сильный дух
Что не даёт
Свернуть с дороги мне в трясину
За то что я ещё могу
Тебе свою подставить спину.

The day of Thanksgiving

I thank you for all of it,
For the joyful sound of the stream,
For the thunder in the sky,
For the leafs whispering to the wind,
For my dear Home,
For the day, so beautiful…

For those friends
Who fearlessly left the crowd,
For the voice of Truth
That keeps me with you in one knot,
For the strong spirit
That doesn't permit me
To digress from my path and fall into the
swamp.
For making it possible
To stretch my hand for help
And give my back for support.

2013

The Essence

Keep bravely walking through the thorny
woods of life, always finding your path.
Be truthful to it.

Your health is your ammunition and
your white horse, take good care of it.

Your Love is the ticket to your soul,
 keep it free from any impurities.

Do not become too absorbed by the
process, let The Guidance be heard.

2013

I send you thanks

I send you thanks for different things.
…And good, and bad, and those that
stink.
I send you thanks from all my heart
For being bold and drift apart.
I never want to be the same.
I will not shoot before I aim.
I learned the moral so well
I almost sent myself to Hell.
For words of wisdom you discoursed
I send you thanks a second course.
The price I pay for lesson this is huge,
But brings me Light and Peace, that may
be never I would get
Unless that fatal day, we've met.

08/2015

Mysterious threads

Mysterious threads like a web of the
spider,
Are barely seen…
You move through the net,
And reluctantly wonder
If you already there have been.
The answers will never come certain and
clear,
But subtle and gentle,
To keep you in quest.
One day you may figure the maze of the
journey,
And readily go to rest…

04/12/2016

When words are melting

When words are melting in the throat
And thoughts are hard to comprehend,
The brain will switch to a different mode
And recognize familiar scent…,
Familiar touch and feather movements of
lips along my bare skin…
The loving whisper of the fingers
creating music from within.
The soft and tender strokes caressing,
that magically fall in place...
The trusting hands are gently pressing
and holding my surrendering face.

06/24/2016

The Bird's Song

If you stay with me forever
The peace will land on earth.
The petals of beautiful roses will embrace
my heart.
My soul will retain an equilibrium of
harmony, bathing in the delight of your
words.
My body will hold the joy of soothing
pleasure that you bring to me with each
encounter…
…And I will keep wondering
        "Is that real?"

2016

I feel one with you

At the dusk of the day I lay next to you,
And you gently stroking my back.
I feel one with you.
Then, in the silence of the night
The dark shadow of fear envelopes me…
The fear, that you will be taken away
from me…
The birth of the new day brings
happiness,
Waking up in your arms.
…But soon the silence of the night will
fall again…

2016

I Know...

Since childhood through life
Playing dolls and first kisses
Real tears and bristly events
My sisters are carrying a dream of a
lifetime
And nothing this dream can prevent.
The beautiful rider, who does not have
fear,
And ready to save you at once
He knows you well, you can trust him
completely.
You bond into strongest alliance.
His horse is as white as first snow that's
falling
And cruising from hugs of the sky.
You trotting empowered, by being
together
And looking the life in the eye.
It could be an end of the beautiful story,
The vision that haunts us for life.

…. But one day I met him. He came unexpected,
Appeared like stepped off my dream.
My guard and protector, my dad and my brother,
My Love and my rest, I know it's him…

03/31/2017

Morning at the pool...

Stay, do not go… Please stay… Let me enjoy your Light!
Do not go yet… Let me breathe your aroma, let me hear the singing.
Stay, let me see the colors, please do not go…
Let me feel the caressing rays and hear whispering trees…
Please stay, do not go.
Let me relish my Love for a little longer…
I will keep repeating this until tomorrow will not come…

02/2020

Memories

…The snow was falling down with fuzzy daisies. They were joyfully flying around and landing on my eyelashes, extending them… Beautiful, wet flowers on my face and on my hair that was sneaking out from the hood of my coat. Happy, happy moments that I will never forget… I was 13, walking with my dad through the meandering night streets of the Old Town. It was almost a ritual to have a walk with dad in the mesmerizing winter evenings. The street lights are illuminating medieval walls and gothic structures, and you feel the presence of the ages… Surreal stage that takes your breath away. Snowflakes are circling in the clandestine chorus, arranging for us their soft carpet on the ground. We talk and laugh… Beauty, Love and Trust. Blissful times…

02/2020

4 Strangers

He unlocked my young and trusted mind and challenged me to perceive the truth, even if it did not fit in the conformist patterns of society. That became the premise of my life.

His kindness and generosity allowed me to pursue my path…. Keep educating myself, dive into the things that were the most important for me, finding myself!

He helped me to fill in an important gaps in my spiritual quest, by sharing with me secrets and wisdom of life.

He is gifting me with the endless Ocean of Love, healing deep wounds of the past.

03/2020